The CHRISTMAS SUITE COLLECTION

Arrangements of Holiday Favorites for Solo Piano

Sharon Aaronson • Dennis Alexander • Cindy Berry • Tom Gerou
Joyce Grill • Victor Labenske • Mary K. Sallee • Robert D. Vandall

ISBN-10: 0-7390-6272-7
ISBN-13: 978-0-7390-6272-2

Alfred

FOREWORD

Celebrate the special moments of the season with these unique collections of holiday favorites by Sharon Aaronson, Dennis Alexander, Cindy Berry, Tom Gerou, Joyce Grill, Victor Labenske, Mary K. Sallee and Robert D. Vandall.

The Christmas Angels celebrates one of the most enduring images of Christmas—the angels who heralded the birth of Jesus Christ. Each of Dennis Alexander's three arrangements of favorite Christmas carols features the angel theme. "Angels from the Realm of Glory" begins the suite with a trumpet-like fanfare followed by a lyrical melody that builds to a triumphant finale. "Angels We Have Heard on High" is slower and more reflective. "Hark! the Herald Angels Sing" joyfully brings the suite full circle by including the melodies from the other movements.

Christmas Bells paints a musical picture of a timeless Christmas tradition—festive bells! Arranged by Mary K. Sallee, the first carol, "I Heard the Bells on Christmas Day," opens with the rousing peeling of bells as the melody unfolds. Next, "The Bells on the Sleigh to Grandma's House" combines the sound of the horse's clip-clop with "Jingle Bells" and "Over the River and Through the Wood." The final arrangement, "Bells Are Ringing," weaves two lovely tunes: "Ding Dong Merrily on High" and "Ring, Little Bells."

The Christmas Manger takes a closer look at the newborn Christ child through three carol arrangements by Tom Gerou. Traditional harmonies are gently mixed with more contemporary ones throughout the suite. "What Child Is This?" begins with a Satie-like accompaniment that transitions to an extended bass line. "Coventry Carol" is a gentle lullaby featuring the melody in thirds over lush harmonies. "Away in a Manger" brings the suite to a close with a berceuse setting of both the traditional and English melodies of this Christmas favorite.

The Christmas Shepherds, arranged by Victor Labenske, focuses on the shepherds who were with their flocks when they heard the joyous news about the birth of Jesus. "How Great Our Joy" creates an image of the angels' appearance to the shepherds in the fields. "It Came Upon the Midnight Clear" expresses the shepherds' wonder through its simple, yet lyrical, treatment of the melody. "The First Noel" begins and ends like a lullaby with the contrasting middle section portraying the angel's glorious announcement of the King of Israel's birth.

He Is Born!, arranged by Joyce Grill, contains four traditional Christmas melodies originating from European countries: Germany, Poland, France, and England. The arrangements convey some of the many moods of the Christmas season, from gentle reflection to celebration. The suite includes "Good Christian Men, Rejoice," "Polish Lullaby," "Il est ne," and "What Child Is This?"

A Jazzy, Jolly Christmas creatively explores jazz idioms in Victor Labenske's entertaining suite containing two upbeat swing pieces and an exquisite ballad. "Up on the Housetop" features a walking bass line in the left hand with a syncopated right-hand melody. A unique ballad arrangement of "Jolly Old St. Nicholas" contains wonderful, lush jazz harmonies. The suite concludes with a spirited arrangement of "Jingle Bells," featuring a playful syncopated melody that appears in both hands.

The Nativity, arranged by Cindy Berry, captures the celebration of Christmas through expressive melodic pictures and rich stylistic contrasts. Performers and listeners alike will experience the wonder and expectancy of the Advent in the melodious "Still, Still, Still." The lush harmonies of "Lo, How a Rose E'er Blooming" bring thoughts of the newborn Baby Jesus in the manger. Celebrate His birth with a jubilant, Classical-styled arrangement of "Joy to the World."

The Three Kings, arranged by Robert D. Vandall, depicts the story of the Magi as they followed the bright star to Bethlehem on the night Christ was born. "March of the Three Kings" reflects the steady journey of the three wise men through the desert. In "We Three Kings of Orient Are," whole-tone scales and a rocking left-hand accompaniment paint a picture of camels traversing the desert. "O Come, All Ye Faithful" is a triumphant procession celebrating the Christ child.

Three Moods for Christmas captures, with the use of a variety of styles and rich harmonies, some of the emotions that this holiday brings to mind. All three movements of Sharon Aaronson's arrangements of well-known Christmas carols are written in triple meter. Experience the joy of the season with "Carol of the Bells" by starting with a single line that builds to a very powerful conclusion. A lyrical rendition of "What Child Is This?" follows, offering reverence to the Christ Child. The suite joyously concludes with the ever-popular "We Wish You a Merry Christmas."

CONTENTS

The Christmas Angels
1. Angels from the Realms of Glory

Henry T. Smart
Arr. by Dennis Alexander

2. Angels We Have Heard on High

Traditional
Arr. by Dennis Alexander

3. Hark! the Herald Angels Sing

Felix Mendelssohn
Arr. by Dennis Alexander

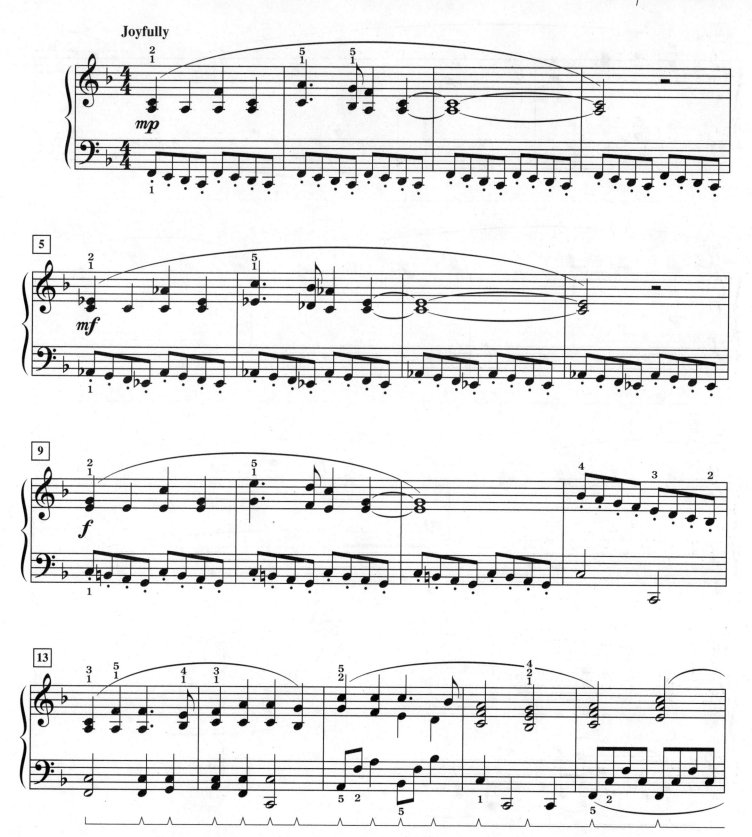

Christmas Bells

1. I Heard the Bells on Christmas Day

Music by John Calkin
Arr. by Mary K. Sallee

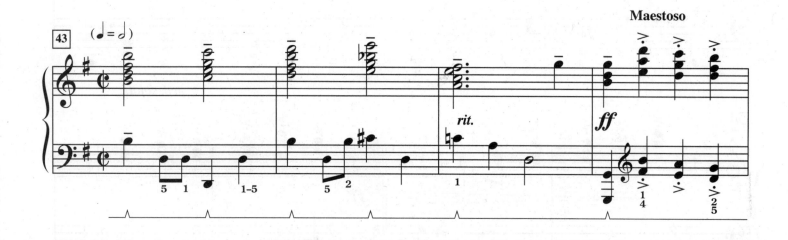

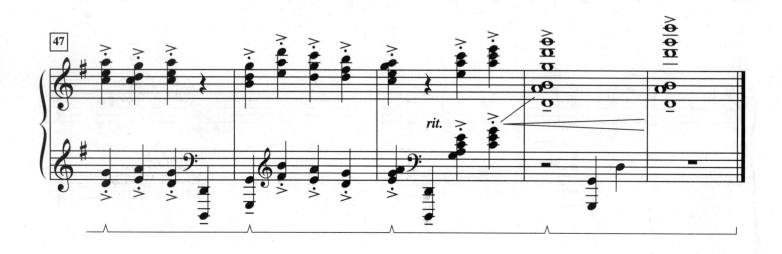

2. The Bells on the Sleigh to Grandma's House

(Over the River and Through the Wood/Jingle Bells)

Arr. by Mary K. Sallee

3. Bells Are Ringing

(Ding Dong Merrily on High / Ring, Little Bells)

Arr. by Mary K. Sallee

Moderato (♩ = ca. 80)

The Christmas Manger
1. What Child Is This?

16th century English melody
Arr. by Tom Gerou

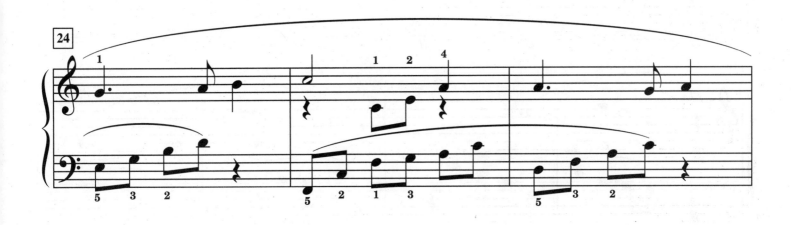

2. Coventry Carol

Traditional
Arr. by Tom Gerou

3. Away In a Manger

William J. Kirkpatrick / James R. Murray
Arr. by Tom Gerou

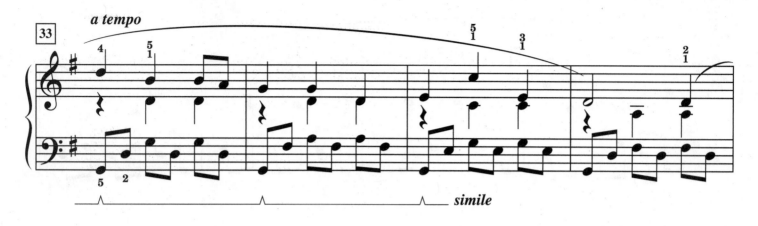

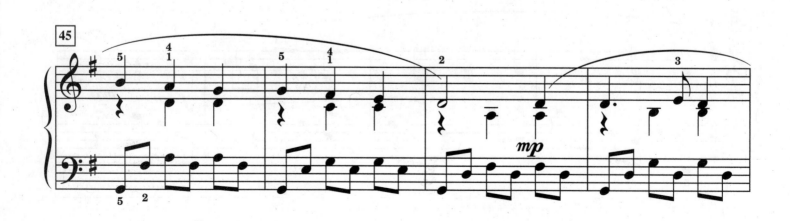

The Christmas Shepherds

1. How Great Our Joy

Traditional German Melody
Arr. by Victor Labenske

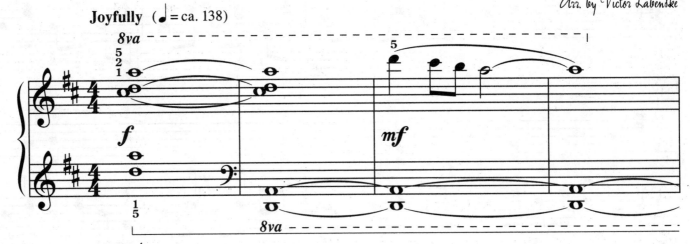

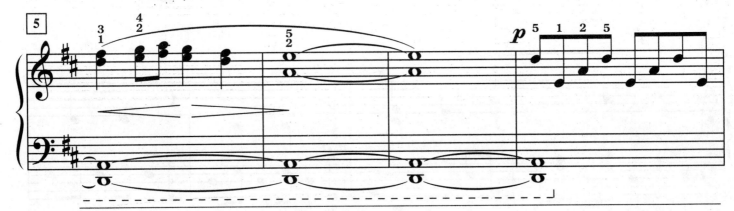

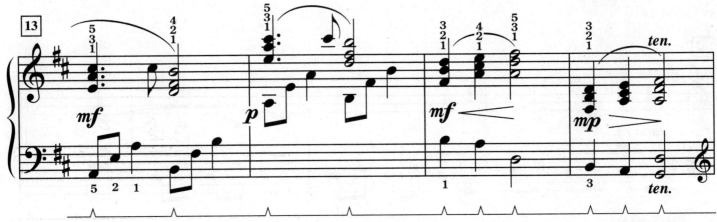

2. It Came Upon the Midnight Clear

Richard S. Willis
Arr. by Victor Labenske

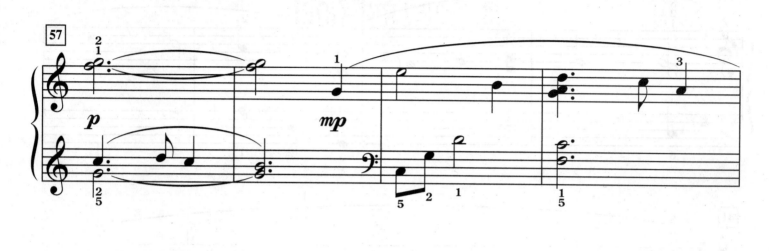

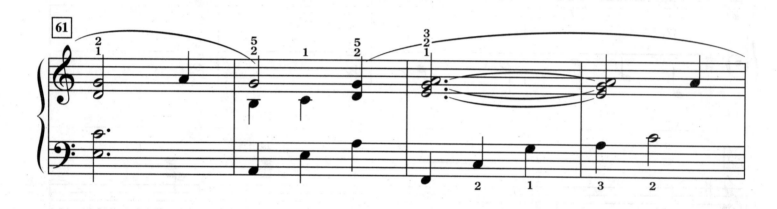

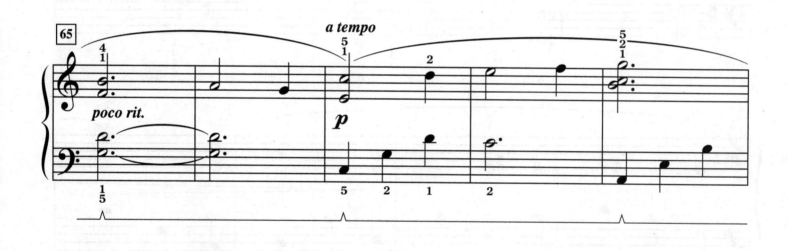

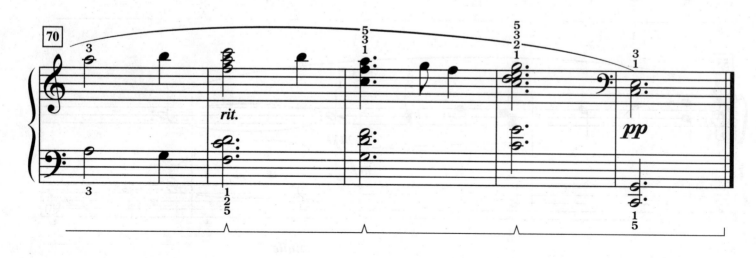

3. The First Noel

Traditional English Carol
Arr. by Victor Labenske

He Is Born!

1. Good Christian Men, Rejoice

14th-century German Melody
Arr. Joyce Grill

2. What Child Is This?

16th-century English Melody
Arr. Joyce Grill

3. Polish Lullaby

Traditional Polish Lullaby
Arr. Joyce Grill

4. Il est ne

Traditional French Carol
Arr. Joyce Grill

A Jazzy, Jolly Christmas
1. Up on the Housetop

Benjamin R. Hanby

Arr. by Victor Labenske

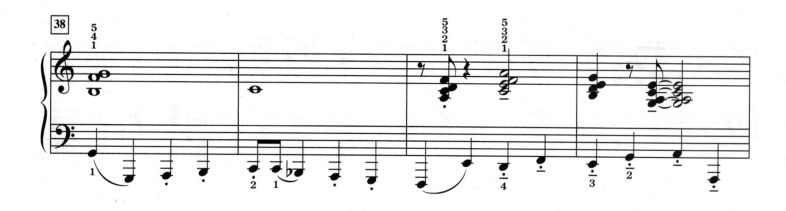

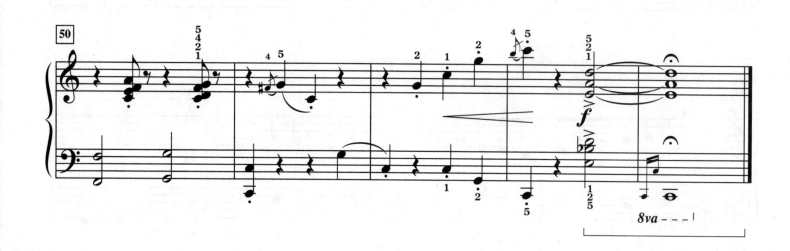

2. Jolly Old St. Nicholas

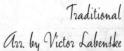

Traditional
Arr. by Victor Labenske

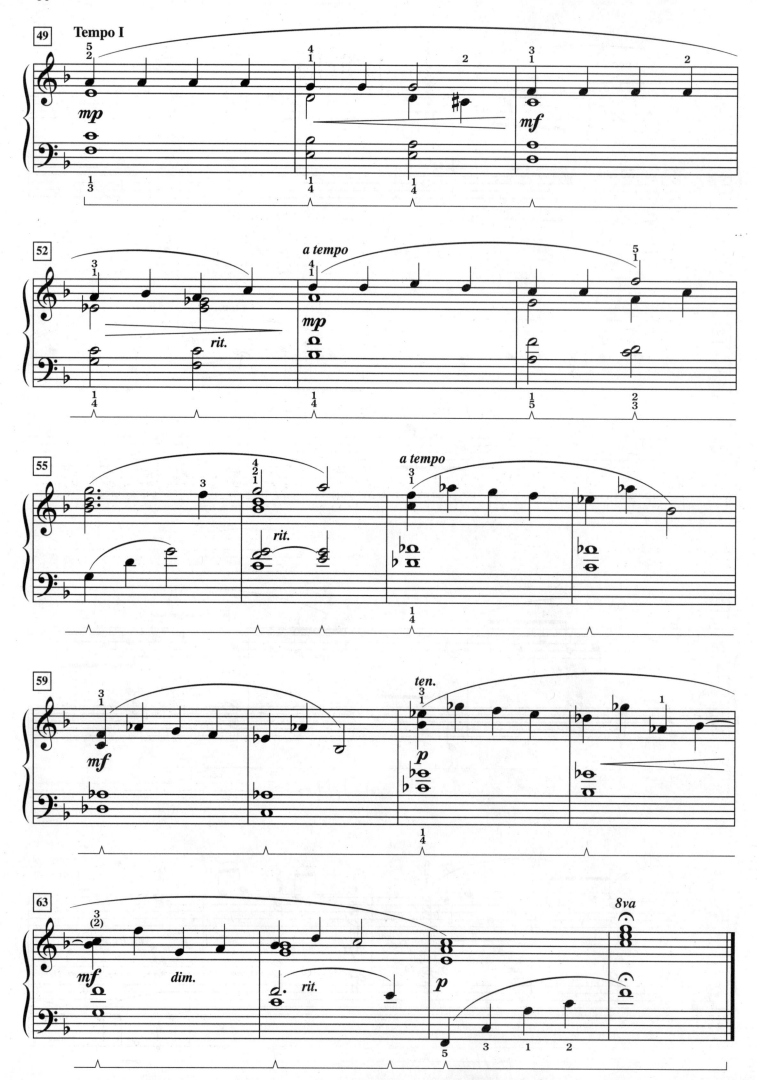

3. Jingle Bells

James Pierpont
Arr. by Victor Labenske

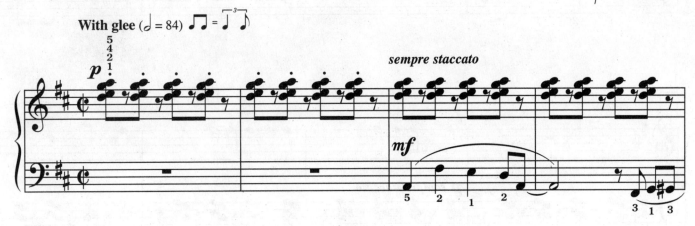

The Nativity
1. Still, Still, Still

Traditional Austrian Carol
Arr. by Cindy Berry

2. Lo, How a Rose E'er Blooming

Words: 15th-century German Carol

Music by Michael Praetorius

Arr. by Cindy Berry

With more motion

3. Joy to the World

Words by Isaac Watts
Music by George Frideric Handel
Arr. by Cindy Berry

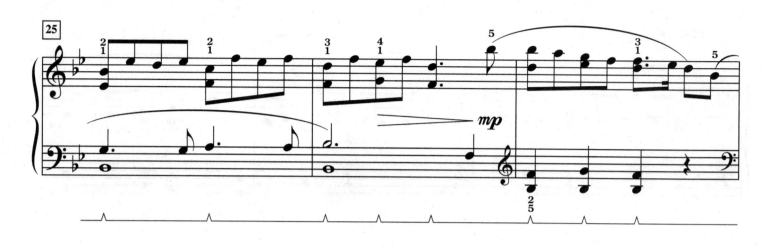

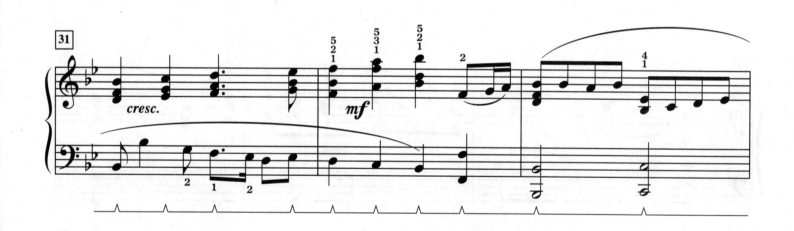

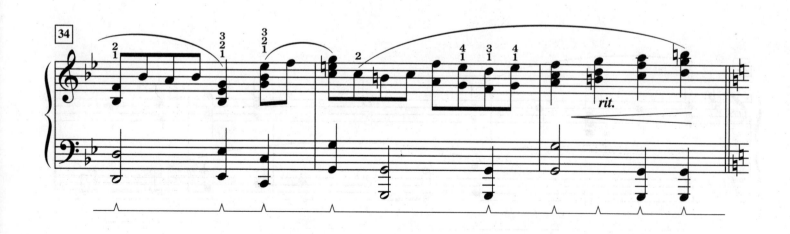

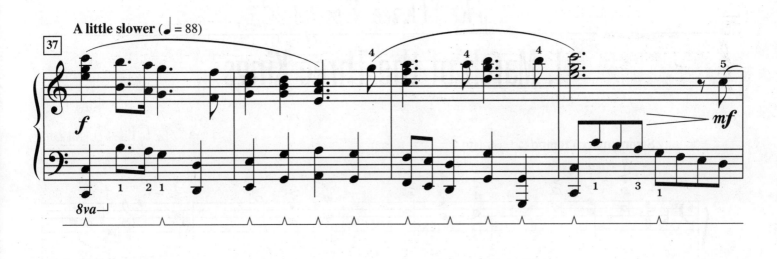

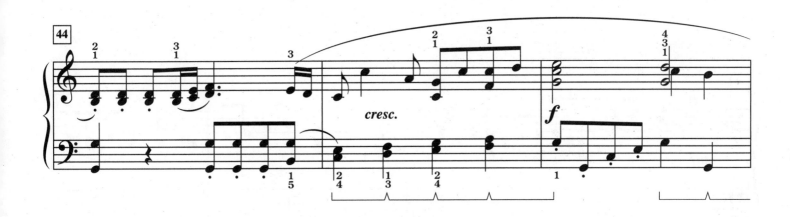

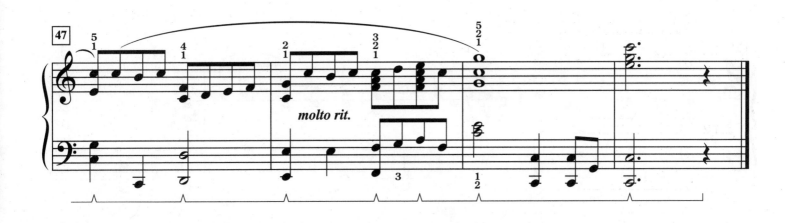

The Three Kings
1. March of the Three Kings

French Carol
Arr. by Robert D. Vandall

2. We Three Kings of Orient Are

John Henry Hopkins, Jr.
Arr. by Robert D. Vandall

Slowly, with expression and freedom ($\bullet$. = ca. 44)

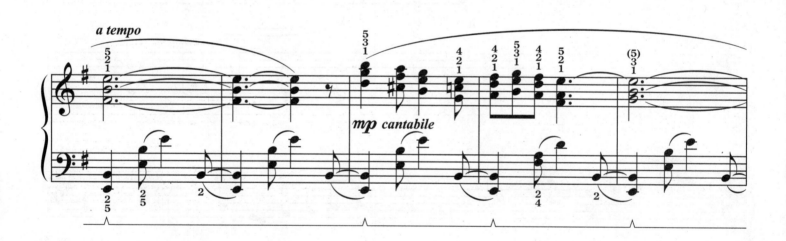

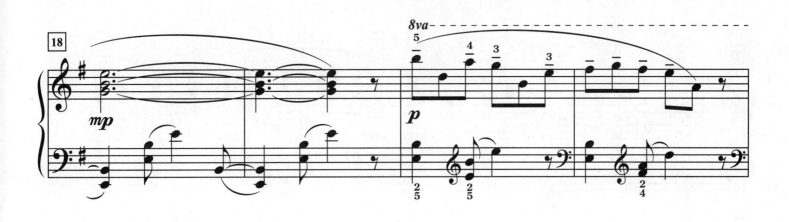

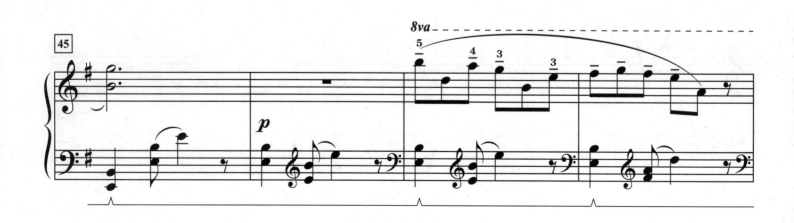

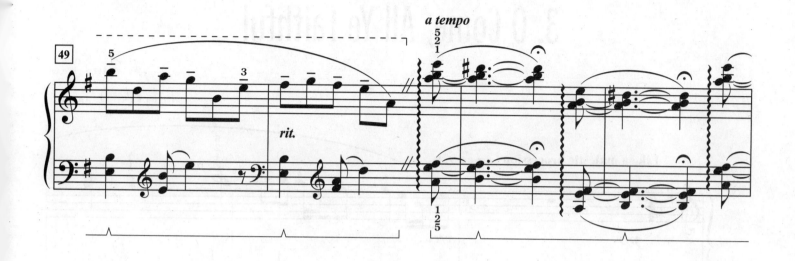

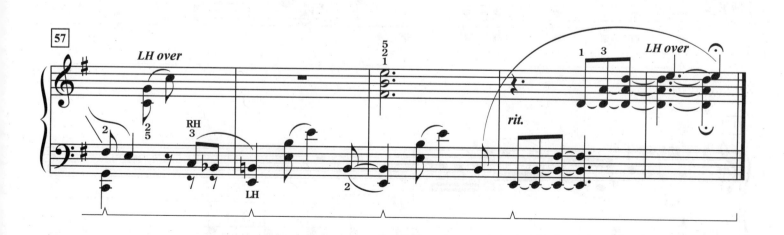

3. O Come, All Ye Faithful

John Francis Wade
Arr. by Robert D. Vandall

Three Moods for Christmas
1. Carol of the Bells

M. Leontovich
Arr. by Sharon Aaronson

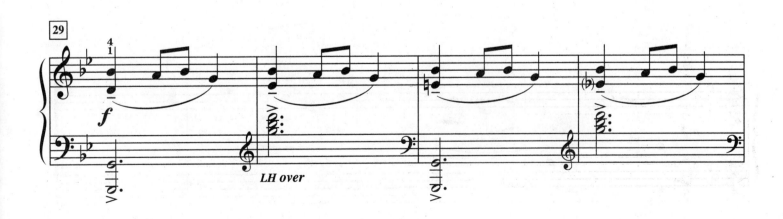

2. What Child Is This?

Old English Melody
Arr. by Sharon Aaronson

3. We Wish You a Merry Christmas

Traditional
Arr. by Sharon Aaronson